copycat candy Bars

Printed in the United States of America
by G&R Publishing Co.

Distributed By:

507 Industrial Street
Waverly, IA 50677

ISBN-13: 978-1-56383-437-0
ISBN-10: 1-56383-437-5
Item #7079

TIPS & TECHNIQUES

For the Best Homemade Candy Bars

✓ Using a heavy saucepan helps eliminate scorching when cooking for long periods of time or at high temperatures.

✓ Candy bars coated in almond bark or candy wafers (candy melts) will set up faster than those coated in other types of chocolate. However, chocolate chips or baking chocolate combined with a small amount of melted vegetable shortening may also be used.

✓ To easily coat candy, set one piece at a time in a bowl of melted coating. Push down to completely cover the candy or drizzle the coating over the top until covered. Lift with a fork and tap the fork against the side of the bowl to remove excess coating. Slide the covered candy off the fork onto waxed or parchment paper.

✓ Recipes list specific chocolate types, but there are so many different flavors and brands to choose from that you can make your candy bars to your liking just by changing it up.

✓ When using a candy thermometer, attach it so the bulb does not touch the bottom of the pan.

300° is hard crack ↗

✓ **For easy substitutions in this book:**
  1 C. chocolate chips or candy wafers ≈ 5 to 6 oz. baking chocolate ≈ ½ C. melted chocolate

3

makes
18

Maple Candy Buns

1 C. milk chocolate chips

1 C. butterscotch baking chips

1 C. creamy peanut butter

1 C. dry roasted peanuts

½ C. butter

¼ C. milk

2 T. vanilla cook & serve pudding mix

3½ C. powdered sugar

½ tsp. maple flavoring

Assembly

1 In the top of a double boiler over medium heat, melt together chocolate chips, butterscotch chips and peanut butter, stirring occasionally. Divide mixture between two small bowls. Stir peanuts into one bowl until well combined. Set aside for 15 to 20 minutes to cool slightly.

2 Line two rimmed baking sheets with waxed paper. Transfer plain chocolate mixture by tablespoonfuls in puddles on waxed paper, spreading each puddle to about 2½˝ in diameter. Freeze until solid.

3 In a medium saucepan over medium heat, melt butter. Add milk and pudding mix, whisking until mixture just begins to boil. Remove from heat and beat in powdered sugar until smooth. Stir in maple flavoring. Set aside to cool slightly.

4 Remove chocolate from freezer and place 1 heaping tablespoon pudding mixture in the center of each chocolate round, spreading nearly to the edge. Place 1 tablespoon set-aside peanut mixture on top of pudding mixture, carefully spreading to the edge.

5 Freeze until solid. Serve frozen or thaw slightly.

Cute. Yes?

makes
18

Heathcliff Bars

1 C. butter, softened

1⅓ C. sugar

2½ T. water

2 T. light corn syrup

1½ C. milk chocolate chips

¾ C. dark chocolate chips

2 tsp. vegetable shortening

Sliced almonds, crumbled, optional

Assembly

1 Line a 9 x 9" baking pan with aluminum foil; butter foil generously and set aside.

2 In a large saucepan over medium heat, heat butter, sugar, water and corn syrup until melted, stirring constantly; scrape down sides of pan and insert a candy thermometer. Cook until mixture reaches 300° (hard crack stage), stirring constantly and reducing heat slightly to keep mixture from boiling over, if necessary. Quickly pour hot mixture into prepared pan; tap pan on counter until top is smooth. Allow toffee to set up for 1 to 2 minutes.

3 Butter a sharp knife and score toffee to indicate cutting lines, firmly cutting through to bottom of pan. If toffee fills the cuts, it's still too hot; wait 30 seconds and try again. Then let toffee cool completely.

4 Lift foil from pan and carefully break toffee apart along scored lines.

5 Spray a wire rack with nonstick cooking spray and set over a piece of waxed paper; set aside. In a medium microwave-safe bowl, combine milk chocolate and dark chocolate chips; melt in the microwave according to package directions, stirring until smooth. Stir in shortening until melted.

6 Coat toffee pieces in melted chocolate and transfer to prepared rack. Run a spoon across top to add texture and sprinkle with almonds while wet, if desired. Let dry for 1 to 2 hours.

makes
16

Munchy Moose Bars

12 oz. vanilla almond bark

12 oz. chocolate almond bark

1 C. milk chocolate chips

⅔ C. bittersweet chocolate chips

1 C. white baking chips

2 tsp. vegetable shortening

1 C. cashews

1½ to 2 (10 oz.) pkgs. Crunch 'n Munch, lightly crushed

Assembly

1 Line a 9 x 13" pan with aluminum foil; spray with nonstick cooking spray and set aside.

2 In a large microwave-safe bowl, melt together vanilla and chocolate almond barks, milk chocolate and bittersweet chocolate chips, white baking chips and shortening in the microwave; stir until smooth.

3 Stir in cashews and as much of the Crunch 'n Munch as possible. Spread evenly in prepared pan.

4 Refrigerate for 1 hour or until firm. Cut into bars.

Now Try This

*Make a snack mix by lining two rimmed baking sheets with foil. Prepare chocolate as directed. Stir in cashews and **uncrushed** Crunch 'n Munch. Spread on baking sheets, separating kernels. Cool and break into pieces. Place in cellophane treat bags, adding other candy, if desired.*

makes **40**

Malted Milk Balls

1¼ C. white baking chips

1⅓ C. malted milk powder

1½ to 2 C. milk chocolate candy wafers

Fun little pop-'em-in-your-mouth treats.

Assembly

1. In a medium microwave-safe bowl, melt white baking chips in the microwave according to package directions; stir until smooth. Stir in malted milk powder until well combined; set aside.*

2. Place candy wafers in a shallow microwave-safe bowl and melt in the microwave according to package directions; stir until smooth.

3. Line a work surface with waxed paper. Roll malt mixture into 1" balls and arrange on waxed paper. If the balls start to flatten, wait a few minutes before rolling more.

4. Coat the balls in melted chocolate and transfer to waxed paper. Let set at room temperature or refrigerate briefly until chocolate is solid.

* *The malt mixture holds a ball shape better after it has set for a few minutes; however, don't wait too long or it will solidify, making it very difficult to roll.*

makes
10

Peanut Butter Cups

8 (1 oz.) squares semi-sweet
  baking chocolate, divided

1⅓ C. semi-sweet or milk chocolate chips,
  divided

2 T. vegetable shortening, divided

½ C. creamy peanut butter

2 T. butter, softened

¼ C. plus 2 T. powdered sugar, sifted

12

Assembly

1 Line 10 standard muffin cups with paper liners and set aside.*

2 In a small microwave-safe bowl, heat four squares baking chocolate in the microwave in 30-second intervals until partially melted. Add ⅔ cup chocolate chips and heat 30 seconds more or until nearly melted. Add 1 tablespoon shortening and stir until shortening and chocolate chips are melted. Divide melted chocolate evenly among liners. Set on a level surface in freezer for 15 minutes or until firm.

3 In a small mixing bowl, beat peanut butter, butter and powdered sugar on low speed until well blended. Divide mixture evenly among liners and spread over chocolate to create a smooth surface. Set in freezer about 15 minutes.

4 Melt remaining four squares baking chocolate, ⅔ cup chocolate chips and 1 tablespoon shortening as directed above. Pour a little chocolate on top of peanut butter layer in one liner. Immediately tap pan on work surface to evenly distribute chocolate, breaking any bubbles with a toothpick. Repeat with remaining chocolate. Freeze for 15 minutes or until set.

5 Refrigerate or bring to room temperature before serving.

* For miniature Peanut Butter Cups, line miniature muffin cups with liners; divide chocolate and peanut butter mixtures evenly among liners as directed above.

What Do You Call It Bars

½ C. brown sugar

½ C. light corn syrup

½ C. creamy peanut butter

2½ T. butterscotch baking chips

3 C. Rice Krispies cereal

3 squares chocolate almond bark

¾ C. semi-sweet or milk chocolate chips

makes
18

1 Spray a 9 x 9˝ baking pan with nonstick cooking spray; set aside.

2 In a medium saucepan over medium heat, stir together brown sugar, corn syrup and peanut butter until mixture is hot and brown sugar is dissolved. Remove from heat; add butterscotch chips, stirring until melted and smooth. Stir in cereal until well coated. Transfer mixture to prepared baking pan, pressing firmly in an even layer. Refrigerate for 20 minutes or until set.

3 In the top of a double boiler over medium heat, melt together chocolate almond bark and chocolate chips, stirring occasionally until blended and smooth. Remove from heat.

4 With a sharp knife, cut chilled cereal mixture into bars. Coat each bar in melted chocolate and transfer to a foil-lined baking sheet. Set aside until firm.

Now Try This

Instead of pressing cereal mixture into a pan, roll into balls and insert a lollipop stick halfway through the center of each. Melt chocolate almond bark (eliminate chocolate chips) and dip "pops" into chocolate. Add sprinkles and enjoy!

makes
40

½ C. honey
½ C. crunchy peanut butter
1 C. instant nonfat dry milk

Little Bits of Honey

A little bit o' honey in every morsel.

1 In a medium microwave-safe bowl, melt together honey and peanut butter in the microwave. Stir in dry milk. Heat an additional 10 to 15 seconds; stir well.

2 When cool enough to handle, knead mixture on a flat work surface until smooth; place on waxed paper. With a rolling pin, roll mixture to about ½″ thickness. With a sharp knife, cut into strips about ¾″ wide; cut strips into 1¾″ pieces. Round off edges of candies, if desired. Set aside to dry.

3 Cut additional waxed paper into 3½ x 6″ rectangles. When candy is dry, wrap each piece in a waxed paper rectangle; twist ends to seal.

Peanutty Butter Fingers

1 (18.5 oz.) bag candy corn
1½ C. creamy peanut butter
1 (14 oz.) pkg. milk chocolate
candy wafers

Super simple and amazingly scrumptious!

makes
18

Assembly

1 Line a 9 x 9″ baking pan with parchment paper, letting ends of paper hang over edges of pan; set aside.

2 Place candy corn in a large microwave-safe bowl and heat in the microwave for 1 minute; stir. Return to microwave, heating in 30-second intervals until melted, stirring until smooth. Immediately stir in peanut butter until well combined, heating 15 seconds longer to soften, if needed. Spread mixture evenly in prepared baking pan. Refrigerate for 1 hour.

3 Remove chilled mixture from pan by lifting ends of parchment paper. With a sharp knife, slice candy into bars.*

4 In a shallow microwave-safe dish, melt candy wafers in the microwave according to package directions; stir until smooth. Coat bars in melted chocolate and transfer to parchment paper. Let set until chocolate hardens.

If candy crumbles, let set at room temperature for 15 minutes.

Now Try This

Make "pops" by following instructions through Step 3, but cut candy into triangles and insert sticks. Coat entire triangle and part of the stick with melted yellow candy wafers. When dry, make stripes with melted orange and white wafers; let dry.

Nutty Rolls

¾ C. butter, divided

4 C. mini marshmallows

2 tsp. clear vanilla extract

½ tsp. salt

4 C. powdered sugar, sifted

4 C. salted dry roasted peanuts, coarsely chopped

1 (14 oz.) pkg. caramels

1 (14 oz.) can sweetened condensed milk

makes
16

Assembly

1 In a medium saucepan over medium-low heat, heat ½ cup butter, marshmallows, vanilla and salt, stirring until melted and smooth. Transfer mixture to a large bowl and add powdered sugar, stirring until well blended.

2 Line a rimmed baking sheet with parchment paper. When marshmallow mixture is cool enough to handle, transfer to a flat work surface and knead until shiny; divide mixture into 16 equal pieces. Roll each piece into a 4″ rope. Arrange ropes on prepared baking sheet and refrigerate until firm, at least 30 minutes.

3 Place chopped peanuts in a shallow dish; set aside. In a clean medium saucepan over medium-low heat, heat caramels, sweetened condensed milk and remaining ¼ cup butter until melted and smooth, stirring often.

4 Dip each chilled rope into melted caramel until completely covered. Lift with a fork and drag the fork against the side of the bowl to remove excess caramel. Set ropes in chopped peanuts; roll until well coated, pressing to adhere. Return coated ropes to baking sheet.

5 Refrigerate for 1 hour or until firm. Cut ropes into smaller pieces, if desired.

Variation: *To make pecan rolls, replace peanuts with pecans and vanilla extract with cherry flavoring, if desired.*

Cherry Smash

1 C. sugar

1 T. butter

¼ tsp. salt

⅓ C. half & half

1½ C. mini marshmallows

1 C. plus 2 T. mini cherry baking chips

2 T. coarsely chopped maraschino cherries (about 8), drained

1 C. creamy peanut butter

4 squares chocolate almond bark, coarsely chopped

1 C. finely chopped salted peanuts

1 In a medium saucepan over medium heat, combine sugar, butter, salt and half & half. Cook until butter is melted and mixture begins to bubble around the edges. Increase heat to medium-high and boil for 5 minutes, stirring occasionally.

2 Remove from heat and add marshmallows and cherry baking chips, stirring until melted. Stir in cherries. Set aside until just cool enough to handle. Roll into 1¼″ balls and set aside.

3 In a small saucepan over medium-low heat, melt together peanut butter and chocolate almond bark; stir until smooth. Stir in peanuts and remove from heat. Let set a few minutes to cool slightly.

4 Put 1 teaspoon chocolate mixture into the bottom of each cup of a silicone brownie pop mold or other silicone mold.* Set one cherry ball on chocolate in mold. Add chocolate around and over ball until just covered; smooth top of chocolate. Place in freezer for 30 minutes.

5 Pop candies out of molds; thaw before serving.

Don't have a silicone mold? Just line an 8 x 8″ pan with parchment paper. Spread cherry mixture in pan and cover with chocolate mixture, spreading evenly. Refrigerate until firm. Cut into squares using a warm sharp knife.

P'mint Patties

¼ C. sweetened condensed milk

2 oz. cream cheese, softened

1 to 2 tsp. peppermint extract

½ tsp. salt

3½ C. sifted powdered sugar, plus extra for rolling

1 C. dark chocolate chips

1 C. dark chocolate candy wafers

makes
25

Assembly

1 In a large mixing bowl, mix sweetened condensed milk, cream cheese, peppermint extract and salt on low speed. Add powdered sugar 1 cup at a time until a stiff dough forms and it is no longer sticky.

2 Shape into 1" balls and roll lightly in extra powdered sugar. Arrange on a parchment paper-lined baking sheet and flatten with the bottom of a glass to about ⅜" thickness. Let dry at room temperature for 2 to 3 hours.

3 In a shallow microwave-safe bowl, melt together chocolate chips and candy wafers in the microwave, stirring until smooth. Let cool slightly.

4 Coat dry candies in melted chocolate and transfer to parchment paper. Drag a spoon across tops to make swirls, if desired. Let dry. Serve immediately or refrigerate until serving time.

makes
8

Mrs. Goodbar

1 C. milk chocolate chips
¼ C. dark chocolate chips
1 T. vegetable shortening
⅔ to ¾ C. Spanish peanuts

1 Line an 8 x 8″ baking pan with waxed paper; set aside.

2 In the top of a double boiler over medium heat, melt together milk chocolate and dark chocolate chips and shortening, stirring until smooth. Stir in Spanish peanuts. Transfer mixture to prepared pan, spread evenly and refrigerate for 30 minutes.

3 Using a sharp knife, lightly score chocolate to indicate cutting lines. Return to refrigerator for 30 minutes.

4 Remove from refrigerator and use a sharp knife to cut along score lines.

Now Try This

Turn your homemade candy into a gift for someone close. Use craft or construction paper, string and your printer or stamps to make a custom wrapper with a special message they'll be sure to remember. Anything goes, so use your imagination.

makes
24

3 Mountaineers

¼ C. dark chocolate chips

1 C. milk chocolate chips

¾ C. white baking chips

1 (7 oz.) container marshmallow creme

1 tsp. vanilla extract

2 T. milk

1 (14 oz.) pkg. milk chocolate candy wafers

Assembly

1 Spray 1¼ x 1¼ x ⅝" silicone molds or ice cube trays with nonstick cooking spray;* set aside.

2 In a small microwave-safe bowl, melt together dark chocolate, milk chocolate and white baking chips in the microwave according to package directions, stirring until smooth.

3 In a medium mixing bowl, combine marshmallow creme, vanilla and milk. Beat on high speed while adding melted chocolate until well combined.

4 Fill prepared molds with marshmallow mixture, smoothing the tops. Chill several hours or until firm.

5 In a shallow microwave-safe bowl, melt candy wafers in the microwave according to package directions. Let cool slightly. Remove marshmallow mixture from molds and coat each in melted chocolate. Transfer to waxed paper and let set until firm.

No silicone molds? No problem. Simply follow instructions through step 3. Line an 8 x 8" pan with waxed paper and spread marshmallow mixture evenly in pan. Chill as directed; remove from pan, slice into squares using a sharp knife and coat in melted chocolate.

makes
50

Chit-Chat Bars

1 C. butter

⅓ C. sugar

1 C. brown sugar

2 C. graham cracker crumbs

½ C. half & half

30 plain crispbread crackers,
such as Schär brand*

1½ C. milk chocolate chips

1½ C. chopped chocolate
almond bark

1 T. vegetable shortening

1 In a medium saucepan over medium heat, melt butter. Stir in sugar, brown sugar, cracker crumbs and half & half; bring to a boil. Reduce heat to medium-low and cook for 5 minutes, stirring constantly.

2 Divide the cooked mixture among 20 of the crackers, spreading evenly to the edges. Immediately stack two frosted crackers, one on top of the other, with frosted sides up, to make 10 stacks. Top each with a plain cracker. With a sharp knife, carefully cut each stack widthwise into five even pieces.

3 In a medium microwave-safe bowl, melt together chocolate chips, chocolate almond bark and shortening in the microwave, stirring until smooth.

4 Line a rimmed baking sheet with waxed paper. One at a time, set cracker pieces on a fork and pour melted chocolate over the top until top and sides are coated. Transfer to prepared baking sheet.

5 Refrigerate until firm.

* If crispbread crackers are unavailable, use 96 Club crackers. Line a 9 x 13" baking pan with ⅓ of the crackers. Spread with half the filling; repeat. Cover with remaining crackers. Refrigerate for 1 hour. Cut into pieces and coat in chocolate as directed above.

makes
20

Milky Way-Outs

1 (1 lb. 4 oz.) pkg. chocolate
   almond bark

1 (11.5 oz.) pkg. milk chocolate chips

1 (7 oz.) container marshmallow creme

6 T. evaporated milk, divided

1 (14 oz.) pkg. caramels, unwrapped

1 Spray 2 x 3 x ¾" egg-shaped candy molds (for large eggs) with nonstick cooking spray;* wipe lightly with a paper towel to remove excess, leaving a thin coating in molds. Set aside.

2 In a small microwave-safe bowl, melt half the chocolate almond bark in the microwave according to package directions, stirring until smooth. With a food-safe paintbrush, heavily coat the inside of prepared molds with melted chocolate; chill.

3 In a medium microwave-safe bowl, melt chocolate chips in the microwave according to package directions, stirring until smooth. Add marshmallow creme and 3 tablespoons evaporated milk; stir until well blended. Fill chilled molds ½ to ⅔ full with marshmallow mixture, spreading to edges; chill.

4 In a separate medium microwave-safe bowl, melt together caramels and remaining 3 tablespoons evaporated milk in 45-second intervals, stirring after each interval, until smooth. Pour a layer of caramel over the center of the chilled mixture, filling molds nearly to the top; chill.

5 In the small bowl, melt remaining half of chocolate almond bark, stirring until smooth; let cool slightly. Fill chilled molds with melted chocolate, spreading evenly; refrigerate until solid and remove from molds.

No molds? No problem. Simply line an 8 x 8" pan with foil and spray with nonstick cooking spray. Spread marshmallow mixture evenly in pan and chill. Spread caramel mixture over chilled layer. Chill several hours, cut into squares and dip into melted chocolate almond bark.

makes
12

Chunky-Chunks

½ C. raisins, coarsely chopped

½ C. salted peanuts, cashews and/or filberts, coarsely chopped

2 squares chocolate almond bark

1 C. semi-sweet chocolate chips

Assembly

1 Spray 1¼ x 1¼ x ⅝" silicone molds or ice cube trays with nonstick cooking spray;* wipe lightly with a paper towel to remove excess, leaving a thin coating in molds. In a bowl, toss together raisins and nuts. Set aside.

2 In a medium microwave-safe bowl, melt together chocolate almond bark and chocolate chips in the microwave, stirring until blended and smooth. Stir in raisin mixture until well coated.

3 Divide chocolate mixture evenly among prepared molds, smoothing tops with the back of a spoon. Tap on counter to settle.

4 Refrigerate for 20 to 30 minutes or until firm and remove from molds.

* Or simply spread mixture into a small pan that has been sprayed with cooking spray. Refrigerate and cut into squares.

makes
24

Fake 5 Bars

24 square pretzels

¼ C. creamy peanut butter

12 caramels

1½ tsp. water

¼ C. chopped peanuts

2 C. milk chocolate or dark chocolate candy wafers

1 Arrange pretzels on a parchment paper-lined baking sheet. Place about ½ teaspoon peanut butter on each pretzel and spread evenly with a butter knife.

2 In the top of a double boiler over medium-low heat, melt caramels with water, stirring until smooth.* Working with one pretzel at a time, pour about ¼ teaspoon hot caramel in the center of peanut butter. Immediately sprinkle with about ½ teaspoon peanuts, pressing down lightly to adhere. Set aside until caramel is solid.

3 In a small microwave-safe bowl, melt candy wafers in the microwave according to package directions; stir until smooth. Set a pretzel on a fork and hold above melted chocolate. With a spoon, pour chocolate over top and sides of pretzel until coated. Transfer to parchment paper. Repeat with remaining pretzels. Let set until firm.

* Alternately, melt caramels with water in a small microwave-safe bowl in the microwave at 50 percent power and continue as directed. As caramel begins to set, additional heating will be necessary to keep the caramel pourable.

Twixters

2 C. butter, softened, divided

1 C. powdered sugar

2 tsp. vanilla extract

2 C. flour

1 C. brown sugar

¼ C. light corn syrup

1 C. sweetened condensed milk

1½ C. milk chocolate chips*

1½ C. chopped chocolate almond bark*

2 tsp. vegetable shortening

* Or try white baking chips and vanilla almond bark.

makes
56

1 Preheat oven to 300°. Spray a 9 x 13" baking pan with nonstick cooking spray; set aside.

2 In a medium bowl, beat together 1 cup butter, powdered sugar and vanilla until creamy. Gradually add flour, beating until mixture comes together. With your fingers, press dough firmly and evenly into prepared pan, dusting your fingers with flour to prevent sticking, if needed. With a fork, prick crust all over to eliminate bubbles. Bake for 35 to 45 minutes or until crust is light golden brown in the middle and darker golden brown around the edges.

3 Remove pan from oven and immediately run a knife around the edges to loosen crust. Set aside to cool completely.

4 In a medium saucepan over medium heat, combine remaining 1 cup butter, brown sugar, corn syrup and sweetened condensed milk, stirring constantly until mixture boils; boil for 5 minutes while stirring. Pour over crust and spread evenly. Refrigerate for 30 minutes or until firm.

5 With a sharp knife, cut chilled mixture into bars. Refrigerate for 1 hour.

6 In the top of a double boiler over medium heat, melt together chocolate chips, chocolate almond bark and shortening, stirring until smooth; let cool slightly. Coat chilled bars in melted chocolate and transfer to a waxed paper-lined baking sheet; let set or refrigerate until firm.

Cocoa Mallow Cups

1 C. semi-sweet or milk
  chocolate chips

1 C. milk chocolate
  candy wafers

¼ C. sweetened flaked
  coconut, coarsely chopped

¾ C. marshmallow creme

makes
24

Assembly

1 Line mini muffin cups with liners and set aside.

2 In a medium microwave-safe bowl, melt together chocolate chips and candy wafers in the microwave, stirring until smooth. Stir in coconut until well coated.

3 With a small spoon, spread a thin layer of the chocolate mixture over the bottom and ¾ of the way up the sides of liners; chill for 10 minutes or until set. Set aside remaining chocolate.

4 Transfer marshmallow creme to a zippered plastic bag and cut off one corner; pipe into chocolate cups, leaving about ¼" of chocolate above marshmallow creme.

5 Spoon remaining chocolate mixture over marshmallow filling, spreading to edges to seal. Tap tray against counter to smooth out chocolate.

6 Refrigerate until set.

Tip: *Before measuring marshmallow creme, lightly spray measuring cup and plastic bag with nonstick cooking spray to prevent sticking.*

Double Zero Bars

1 egg white

1 tsp. light corn syrup

2 T. honey

½ tsp. unsweetened cocoa powder

1 T. malted milk powder

1¾ C. powdered sugar

½ tsp. salt

2 T. plus 1 tsp. water, divided

¼ C. chopped peanuts, toasted*

½ C. chopped almonds, toasted*

¾ C. caramel bits

9 squares vanilla almond bark

makes
22

Assembly

1 Line a loaf pan with aluminum foil, letting ends of foil hang over edges of pan; generously grease bottom and 1" up sides of foil with butter. In a medium glass bowl, beat egg white using a whisk attachment on high speed until stiff. Set aside.

2 In a small saucepan, stir together corn syrup, honey, cocoa powder, malted milk powder, powdered sugar, salt and 2 tablespoons water. Insert a candy thermometer and cook over medium-low heat until mixture reaches 275° (soft crack stage), stirring frequently. Immediately remove from heat. With mixer on medium speed, slowly drizzle hot liquid over egg whites. Scrape sides of bowl and beat until nougat mixture begins to stiffen. Immediately stir in nuts using a wooden spoon. Press evenly into prepared pan. Press a piece of buttered foil on top of nougat; set aside to cool.

3 When nougat is cool, remove top foil. In a small microwave-safe bowl, combine caramel bits and remaining 1 teaspoon water. Microwave in 15-second intervals until melted; stir until smooth. Let cool a few minutes, and then spread evenly over nougat in pan. Set aside until caramel is firm.

4 Remove candy from pan by lifting foil. Cut into bars and arrange on a waxed paper-lined tray. Freeze for 15 minutes or until chilled.

5 Melt vanilla almond bark in a shallow microwave-safe bowl in the microwave according to package directions. Coat chilled bars in melted almond bark and return to lined tray; set aside until firm. Drizzle extra bark over the top, if desired.

* To toast, place nuts in a single layer in a dry skillet over medium heat for 6 to 8 minutes or until golden brown; set aside.

Tortoise Candies

60 pecan halves

12 caramels, unwrapped

1 (1 oz.) square semi-sweet baking chocolate

2 squares chocolate almond bark

makes **12**

Assembly

1 Preheat oven to 300°. Line a rimmed baking sheet with aluminum foil, shiny side up. Lightly spray foil with nonstick cooking spray.

2 Arrange pecan halves in clusters of five on prepared baking sheet, with narrower ends of pecans touching in the center, representing a tortoise head and legs. Place one caramel in the center of each cluster. Bake for 9 to 10 minutes or until caramels are soft and pecans are lightly toasted.

3 Remove baking sheet from oven and immediately flatten caramels with the back of a spoon that has been sprayed with cooking spray. If pecans move when flattening caramel, simply push together; set aside.

4 In a small microwave-safe bowl, melt together baking chocolate and chocolate almond bark in the microwave, stirring until smooth. Pour melted chocolate over caramel until caramel is covered; let set until firm.

5 Remove from baking sheet and store refrigerated in an airtight container. Bring to room temperature before serving.

Note: *For an updated flavor, sprinkle a bit of coarse salt over chocolate while wet.*

makes
8

Symphonic Bars

3 (1 oz.) squares semi-sweet baking
  chocolate, coarsely chopped

1⅓ C. milk chocolate candy wafers

½ C. English toffee bits

¼ C. sliced almonds, broken

Assembly

1 Line an 8 x 8" baking pan with aluminum foil and spray with nonstick cooking spray; set aside.

2 In a microwave-safe bowl, melt together baking chocolate and candy wafers in the microwave, stirring until smooth. Add toffee bits and almonds; stir until well coated.

3 Spread mixture evenly in prepared pan. Let set until firm. Cut into bars.

Now Try This

For another popular crunchy bar, replace toffee bits and almonds with ¾ cup Rice Krispies cereal.

makes
20

Snicker-Snackers

2 C. coarsely chopped milk chocolate candy wafers, divided

½ C. milk chocolate chips, divided

¾ C. creamy peanut butter, divided

¼ C. butter

1 C. sugar

½ C. evaporated milk, divided

1½ C. marshmallow creme

1½ C. salted dry roasted peanuts, coarsely chopped

1 tsp. vanilla extract

3 (5.5 oz.) bags chewy caramels, such as Werther's brand

1 Line a 9 x 13" baking pan with aluminum foil, letting ends of foil hang over edges of pan; spray with nonstick cooking spray. Set aside.

2 In a small microwave-safe bowl, melt together 1 cup candy wafers, ¼ cup chocolate chips and ¼ cup peanut butter in the microwave, stirring until smooth. Spread evenly over the bottom of prepared pan. Refrigerate until chocolate is hard.

3 In a medium saucepan over medium heat, melt butter. Stir in sugar and ¼ cup evaporated milk until dissolved. Bring to a boil and boil for 5 minutes, stirring occasionally. Add marshmallow creme and ¼ cup peanut butter, stirring until smooth. Remove from heat and stir in chopped peanuts and vanilla until well mixed. Spread evenly over chilled chocolate. Refrigerate until chilled.

4 In a medium saucepan over low heat, heat caramels and remaining ¼ cup evaporated milk until caramels are melted and mixture is smooth, stirring occasionally. Spread evenly over chilled nougat. Refrigerate until chilled.

5 In a small microwave-safe bowl, melt together remaining 1 cup candy wafers, ¼ cup chocolate chips and ¼ cup peanut butter in the microwave, stirring until smooth. Cool for 5 minutes. Spread evenly over chilled caramel. Refrigerate for 1 hour. Remove candy from pan by lifting foil. Cut into bars.

Note: *Melt additional candy wafers and dip sides of bars into chocolate, if desired.*

Almond Joyfuls

1 (14 oz.) pkg. sweetened flaked coconut

5 oz. sweetened condensed milk

1 tsp. clear vanilla extract

¼ tsp. salt

2 C. powdered sugar

36 whole almonds

2 C. milk chocolate chips

3 T. vegetable shortening

makes
36

Assembly

1 Line a rimmed baking sheet with waxed paper and set in freezer. Place coconut in a food processor and pulse to chop slightly; set aside.

2 In a large bowl, stir together sweetened condensed milk, vanilla and salt. Gradually add powdered sugar, stirring until well blended. Stir in coconut until evenly coated. Shape coconut mixture into 1 x 1½″ bars and arrange on chilled baking sheet. Place an almond on top of each bar, pressing gently to adhere. Refrigerate while preparing chocolate.

3 In a shallow microwave-safe bowl, melt chocolate chips in the microwave according to package directions. Add shortening, stirring until melted; let cool slightly. Coat coconut bars in chocolate and return to baking sheet.

4 Refrigerate until firm.

Variation: *Omit almonds and replace the milk chocolate chips with dark chocolate chips for a different type of candy, because sometimes you just don't feel like a nut!*

Munchy Nut Bars

2 C. salted dry roasted peanuts
½ C. butter
½ C. sugar
¼ C. light corn syrup
1 tsp. vanilla extract

makes
15

Assembly

1 Spread peanuts in an 8 x 8" baking pan and set in a cold oven. Heat oven to 300°.

2 In a medium saucepan over medium-low heat, combine butter, sugar and corn syrup. Insert a candy thermometer and cook until mixture reaches 300° (hard crack stage), stirring constantly.

3 Remove from heat and stir in vanilla. Add warm peanuts, stirring until evenly coated. Return mixture to baking pan and spread evenly with the back of a spoon. Let set 10 to 15 minutes.

4 With a sharp knife, score mixture to indicate cutting lines; let cool. Break apart along scored lines.

Mint Thins

1½ C. semi-sweet chocolate chips, divided

½ C. milk chocolate chips, divided

¾ C. sweetened condensed milk, divided

1 tsp. vegetable shortening

1 C. white baking chips

2½ tsp. peppermint extract

Green food coloring

makes
32

1 Line an 8 x 8" pan with aluminum foil; spray with nonstick cooking spray and set aside.

2 In a small saucepan over low heat, melt together ¾ cup semi-sweet chocolate chips, ¼ cup milk chocolate chips, ¼ cup sweetened condensed milk and shortening, stirring until smooth. Spread mixture evenly in prepared pan. Chill for 5 to 10 minutes.

3 In a separate small saucepan over low heat, melt together white baking chips and ¼ cup sweetened condensed milk, stirring until smooth. Remove from heat and stir in peppermint extract and food coloring. Spread evenly over chilled chocolate layer.

4 Melt remaining ¾ cup semi-sweet chocolate chips, remaining ¼ cup milk chocolate chips and remaining ¼ cup sweetened condensed milk over low heat, stirring until smooth. Spread evenly over chilled mint layer. Refrigerate about 2 hours or until completely set.

5 Remove candy from pan by lifting foil. Cut into small rectangles.

makes **8**

Cookies & Cream

12 oz. white chocolate baking bar, chopped

2 T. whipping cream

1 tsp. clear vanilla

½ C. chopped plain chocolate wafer cookies

Assembly

1 Line an 8 x 8" pan with aluminum foil; set aside.

2 In a medium microwave-safe bowl, combine chopped baking bar, whipping cream and vanilla. Melt in the microwave according to package directions, stirring until smooth. Carefully fold in chopped cookies until evenly distributed.

3 Transfer mixture to prepared pan. Use your fingers or the back of a spoon to spread mixture evenly. Refrigerate about 1 hour or until firm.

4 Remove candy from pan by lifting foil. Using a sharp knife, cut into bars.

Now Try This

Wrap your candy creations in aluminum foil; then wrap strips of muslin around the bar, mummy-like. Attach googly eyes and you have a cute party favor for your Halloween get-together.

Too cute to be creepy!

makes
18

2 C. creamy peanut butter

2 C. sugar

1 C. light corn syrup

1 C. water

½ C. milk chocolate candy wafers

½ C. dark chocolate candy wafers

6th Avenue

Assembly

1 Line a 9 x 9" baking pan with aluminum foil and spray with nonstick cooking spray. Place peanut butter in a large bowl.* Set aside.

2 In a large saucepan over medium heat, combine sugar, corn syrup and water; bring to a boil, stirring constantly. Scrape down sides of pan. Insert a candy thermometer and cook until mixture reaches 300° (hard crack stage), stirring constantly.

3 Pour hot syrup mixture over peanut butter in bowl and stir quickly and vigorously to mix well (you may want to have someone help stir, as the mixture sets up very quickly). Pour into prepared pan; spread evenly. Let set a few minutes; cut with a sharp buttered knife. Recut often while candy cools.

4 When candy has cooled, lift foil from pan and recut to separate the pieces; place on waxed paper and let dry.

5 In a microwave-safe bowl, melt together milk chocolate and dark chocolate candy wafers in the microwave according to package directions; stir until smooth. Spread or pipe chocolate over candy bars. Let set until firm.

A metal bowl will become very hot, so be sure to use potholders.

Now Try This

Prepare as directed, omitting chocolate topping. Immediately sprinkle with toasted coconut, pressing lightly to adhere. Cool completely and recut.

100,000 Buck Bars

About 25 caramels, unwrapped
2 C. milk chocolate chips
¾ C. Rice Krispies cereal

Make a batch and you'll feel like a million bucks (or at least 100,000).

makes
25

Assembly

1 Arrange caramels on a waxed paper-lined baking sheet. Use the back of a metal spatula or large spoon to flatten caramels to about ¼″ thickness.* Use your fingers to shape as desired.

2 In a microwave-safe bowl, melt chocolate chips in the microwave according to package directions; stir until smooth. Add cereal and stir until well combined.

3 Coat each flattened caramel in melted chocolate mixture and transfer to waxed paper.

4 Refrigerate until chocolate is solid.

Soften caramels in the microwave first, if necessary.

makes **28**

Ruthy-Babe Miniatures

¼ C. half & half

25 caramels, unwrapped, divided

1 T. light corn syrup

1 tsp. butter

¼ tsp. vanilla extract

1¼ C. powdered sugar, divided

1½ C. milk chocolate chips, divided

1½ C. chocolate candy wafers

1 T. vegetable shortening, divided

1½ tsp. water

1 C. salted dry roasted peanuts

Assembly

1 In a small saucepan over low heat, combine half & half, five caramels, corn syrup, butter and vanilla. Cook until smooth, stirring often. Stir in ¾ cup powdered sugar. Insert a candy thermometer and cook on low heat until mixture reaches 230° (thread stage), stirring often.

2 Remove caramel mixture from heat. Let set for one minute, then add remaining ½ cup powdered sugar and beat on high speed until well blended and very thick. Quickly roll mixture into ¾" to 1" balls and set on waxed paper.

3 Line mini muffin cups with paper liners. In a medium microwave-safe bowl, melt chocolate chips, candy wafers and shortening in the microwave. Stir until smooth. Pour 1 to 2 teaspoons melted chocolate into each liner and press a caramel ball into chocolate.

4 In the top of a double boiler over medium-low heat, combine remaining 20 caramels and water, stirring until melted and smooth. Working with one liner at a time, drizzle ½ to 1 teaspoon hot caramel over ball and cover immediately with peanuts, pressing down lightly to adhere.

5 Pour melted chocolate around and over each candy until covered. Let set until firm.

Index